THIS BOOK BELONGS TO:

DOT TO DOT

DINOSAUR

DOT - TO - DOT

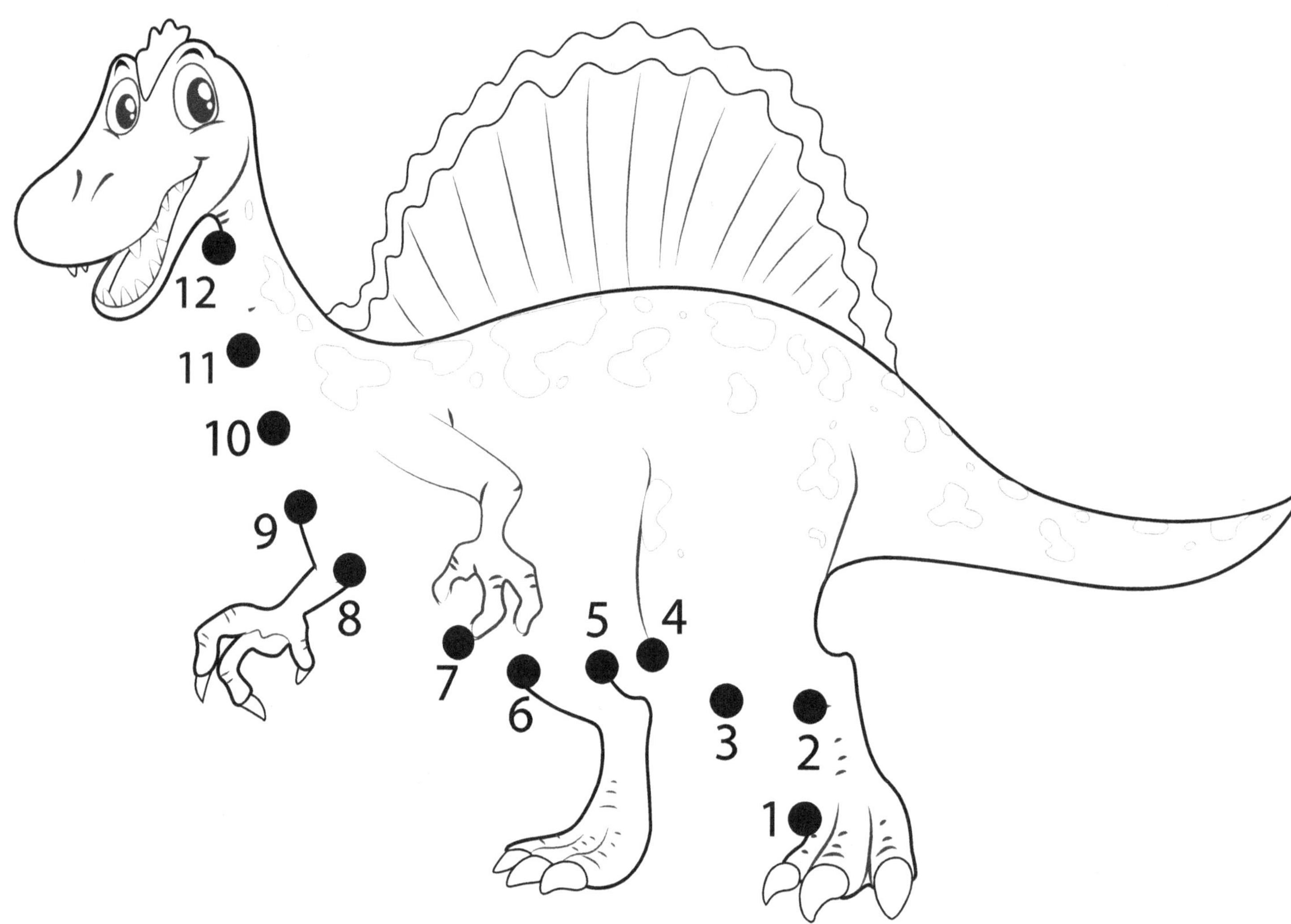

DOT - TO - DOT

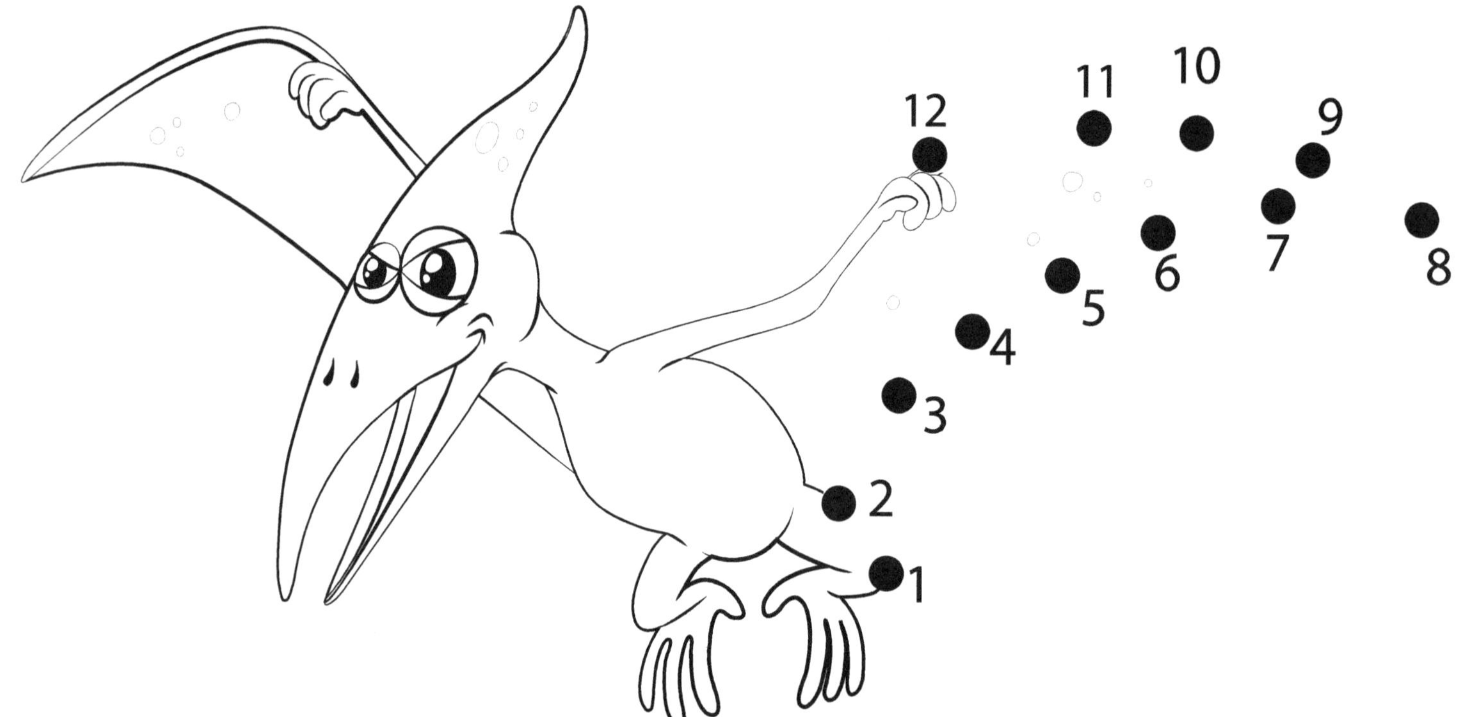

DOT - TO - DOT

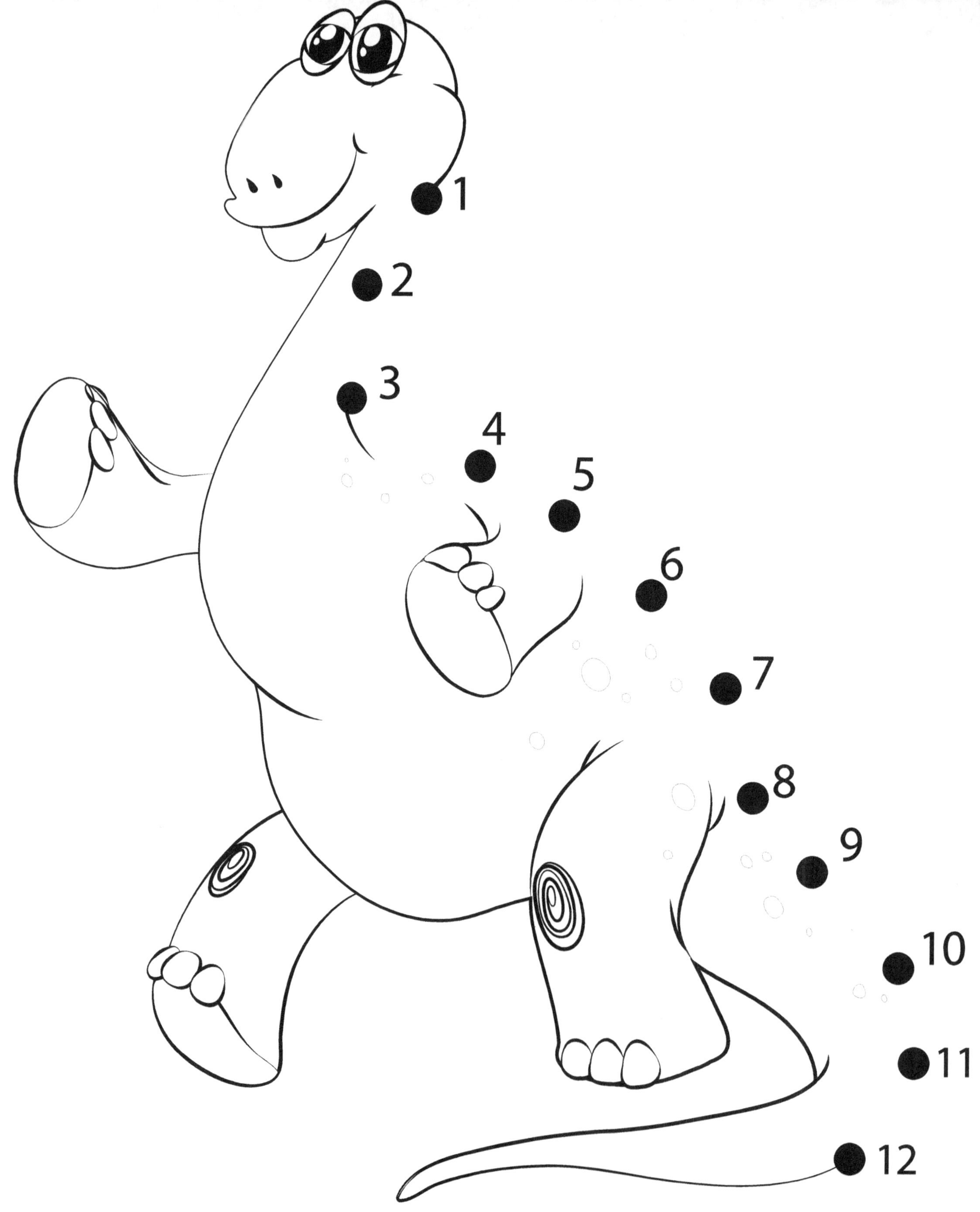

DOT - TO - DOT

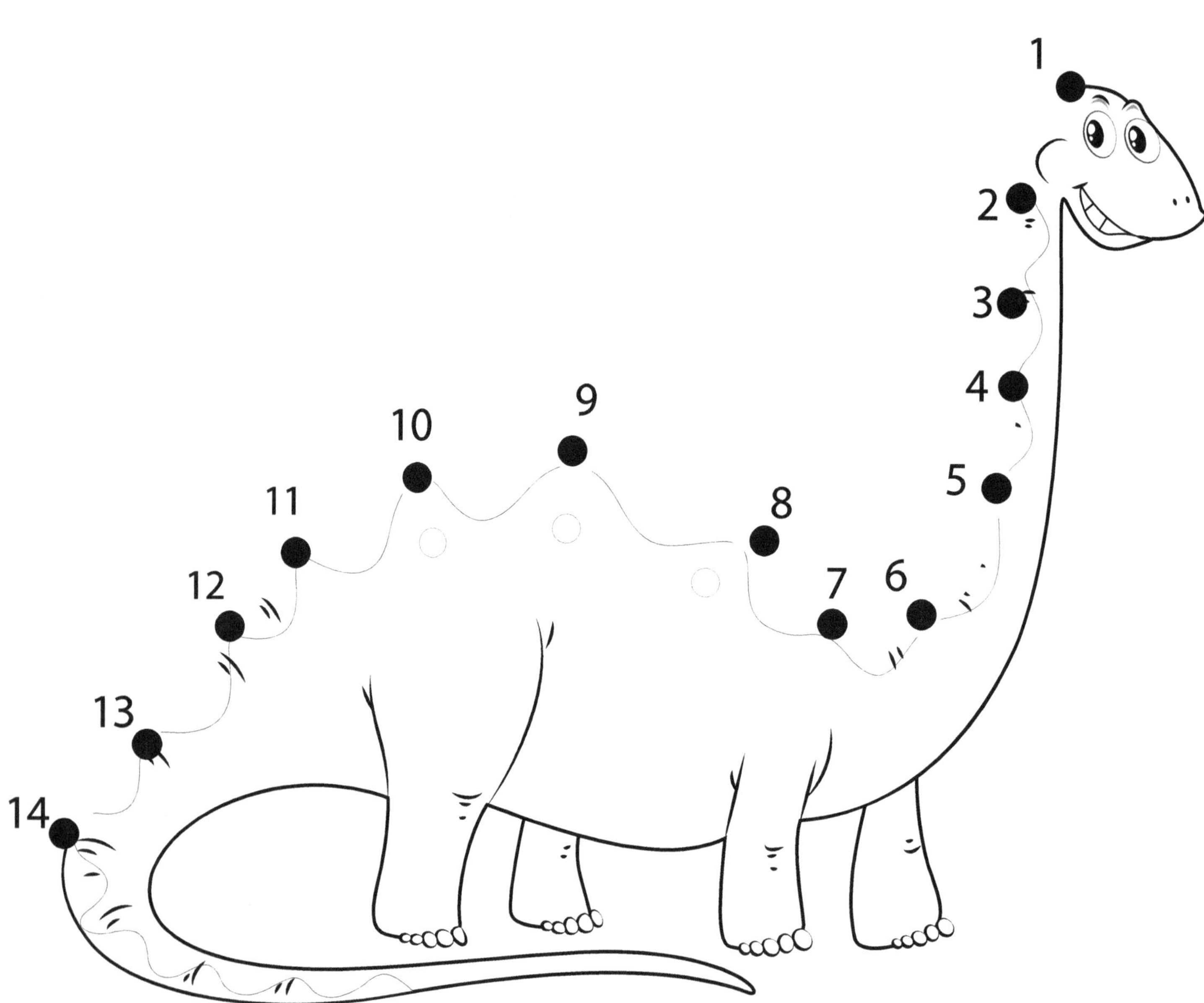

DOT - TO - DOT

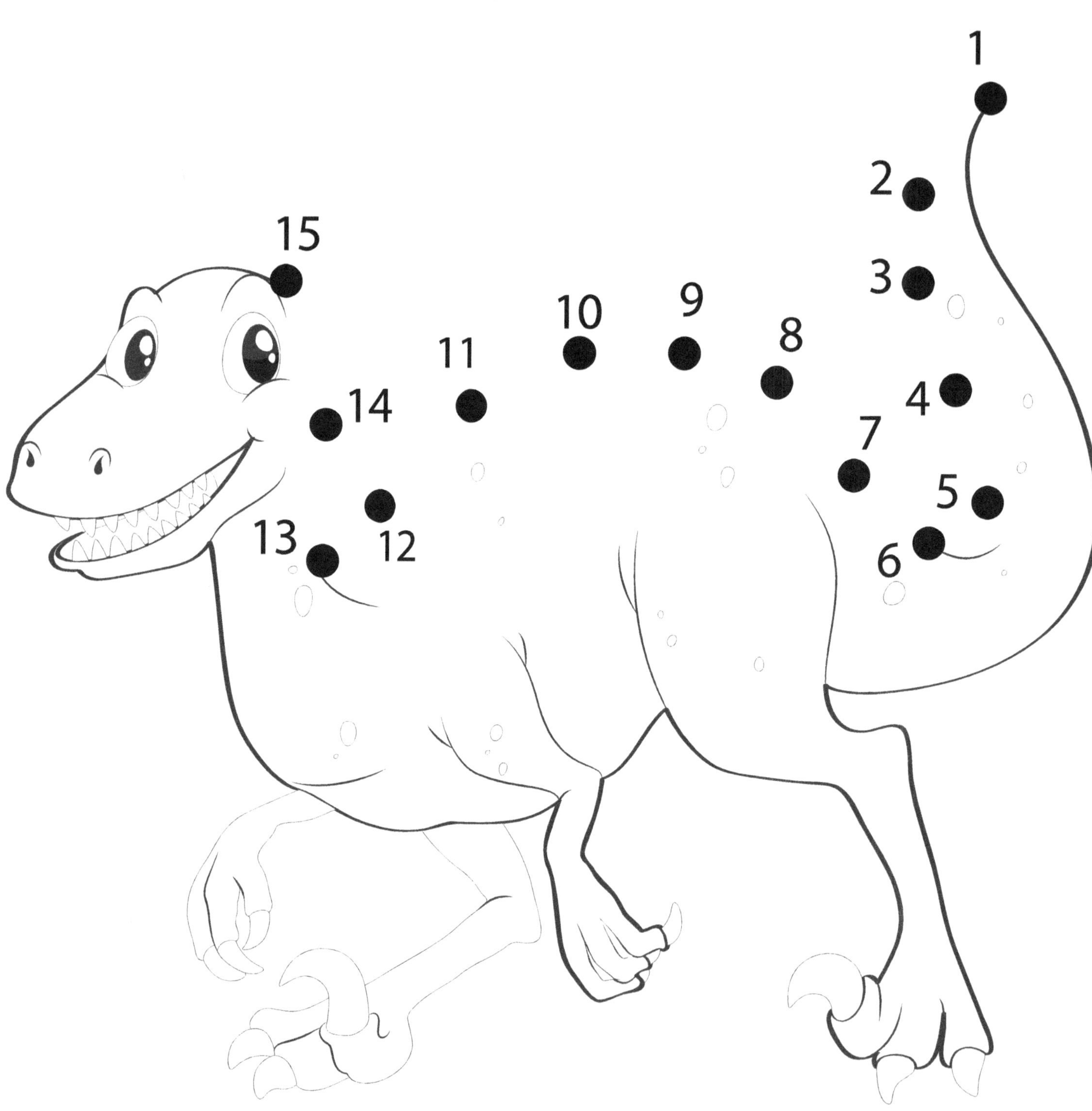

DOT - TO - DOT

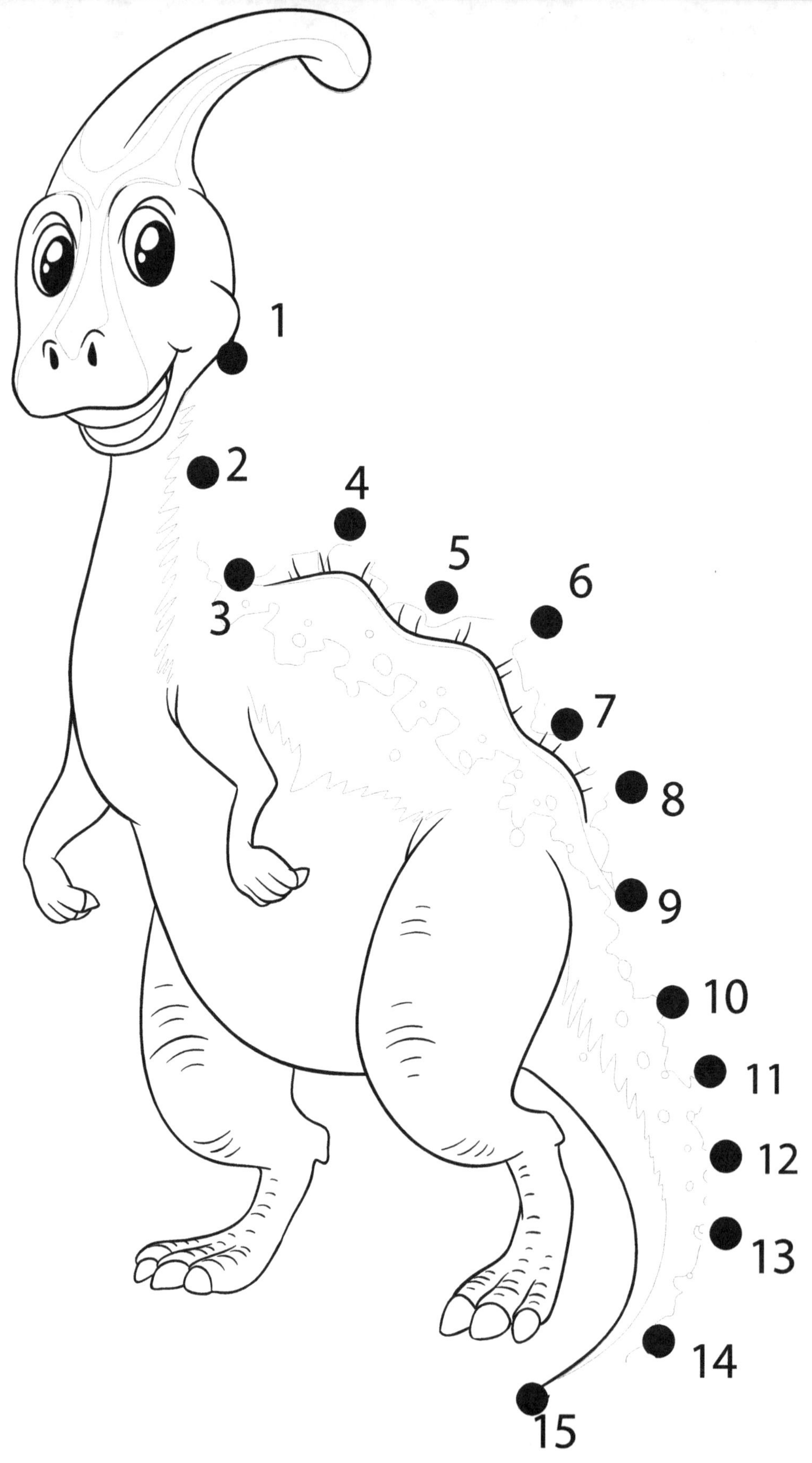

DOT - TO - DOT

DOT - TO - DOT

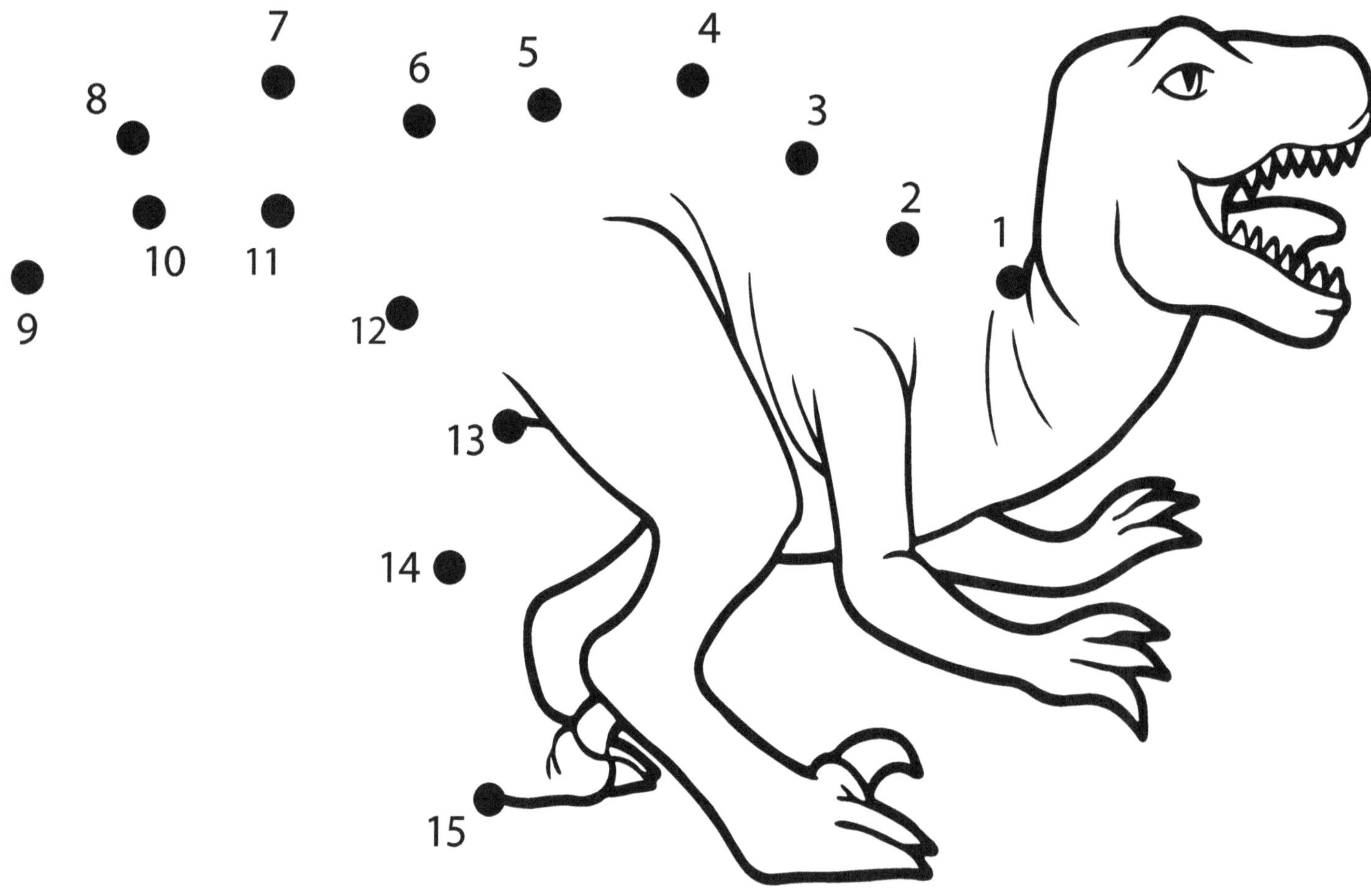

DOT - TO - DOT
1
2
3
4
5
6
7
8
9
10
11
12
13
14
15

DOT - TO - DOT

DOT - TO - DOT

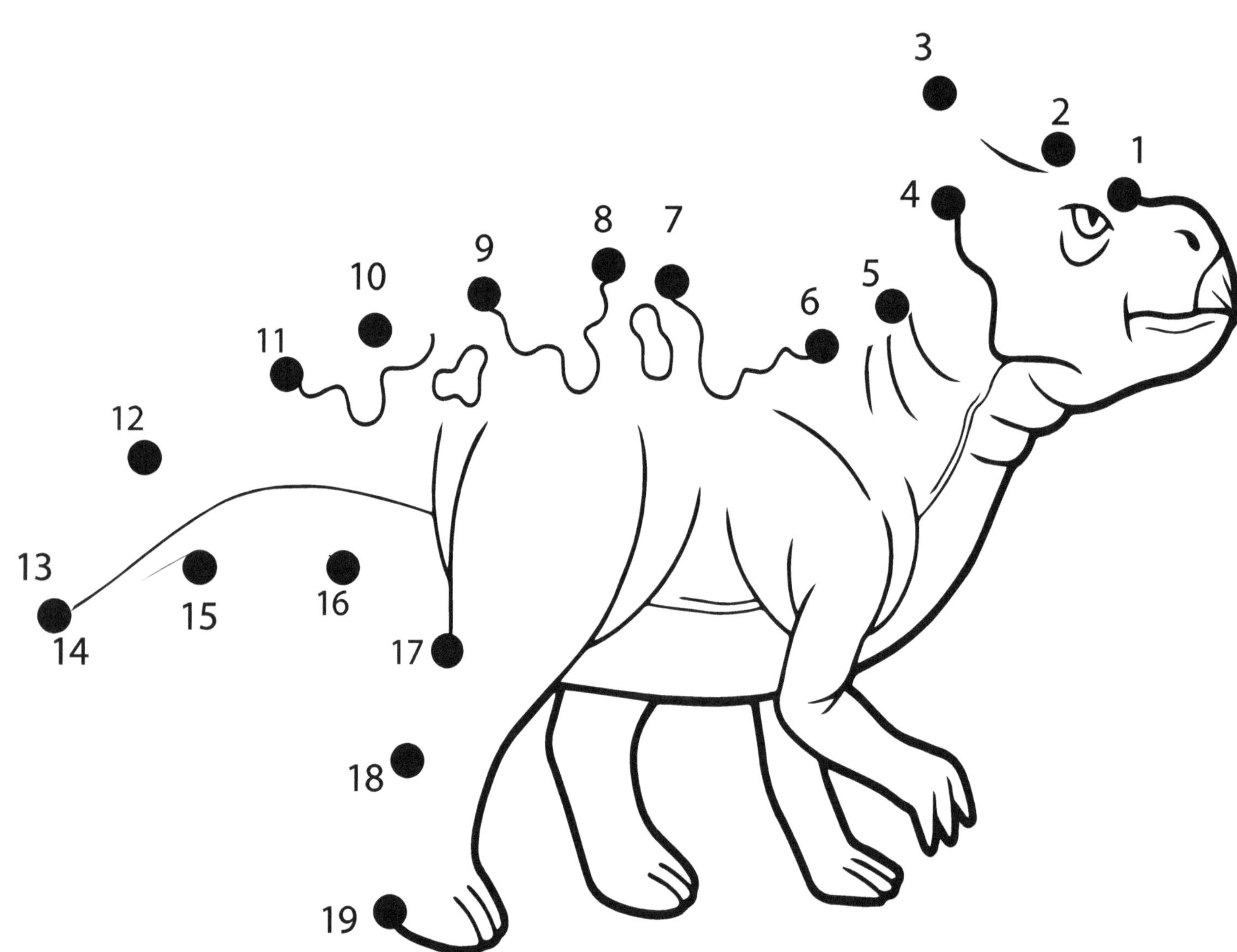

DOT - TO - DOT

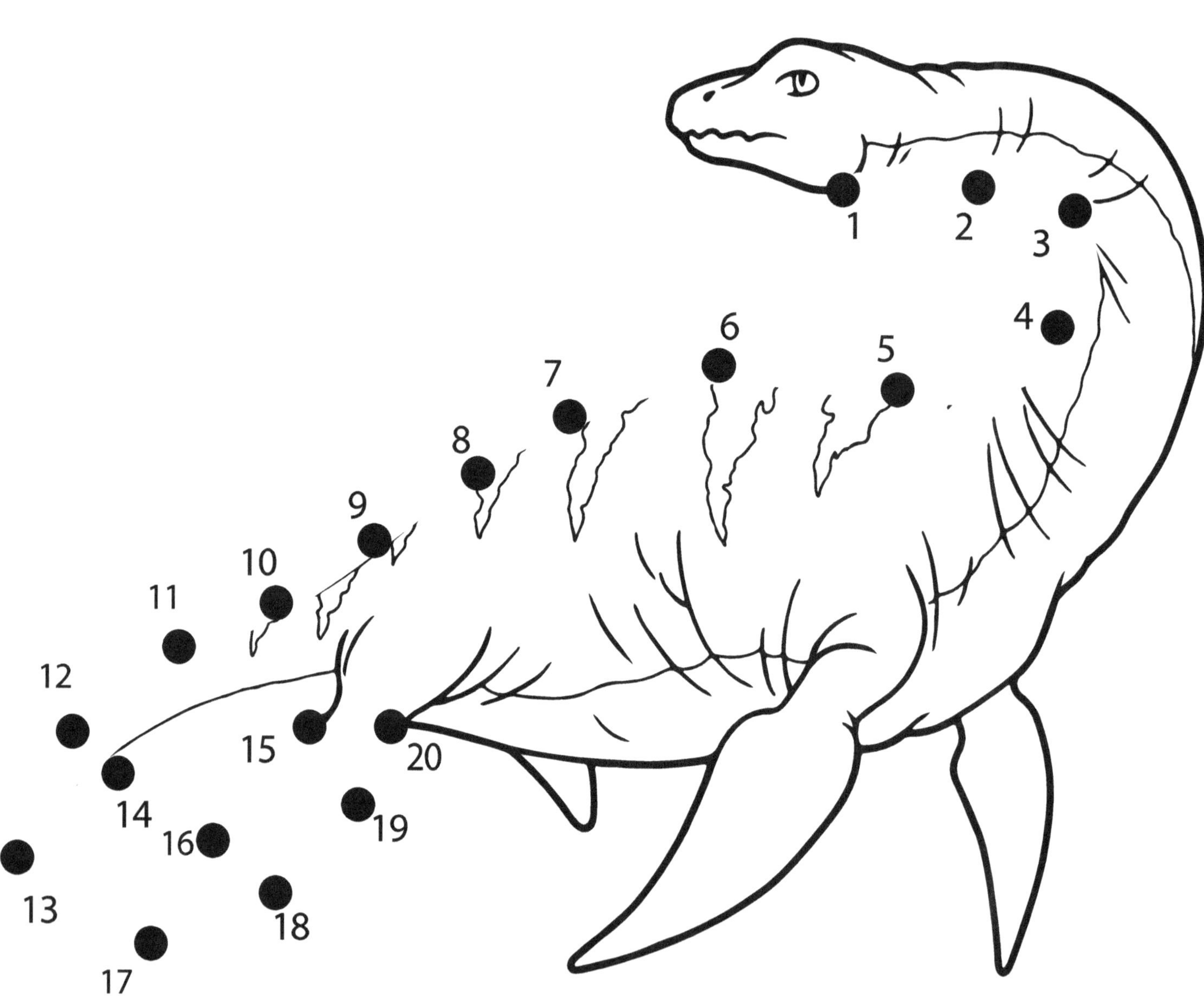

DOT - TO - DOT

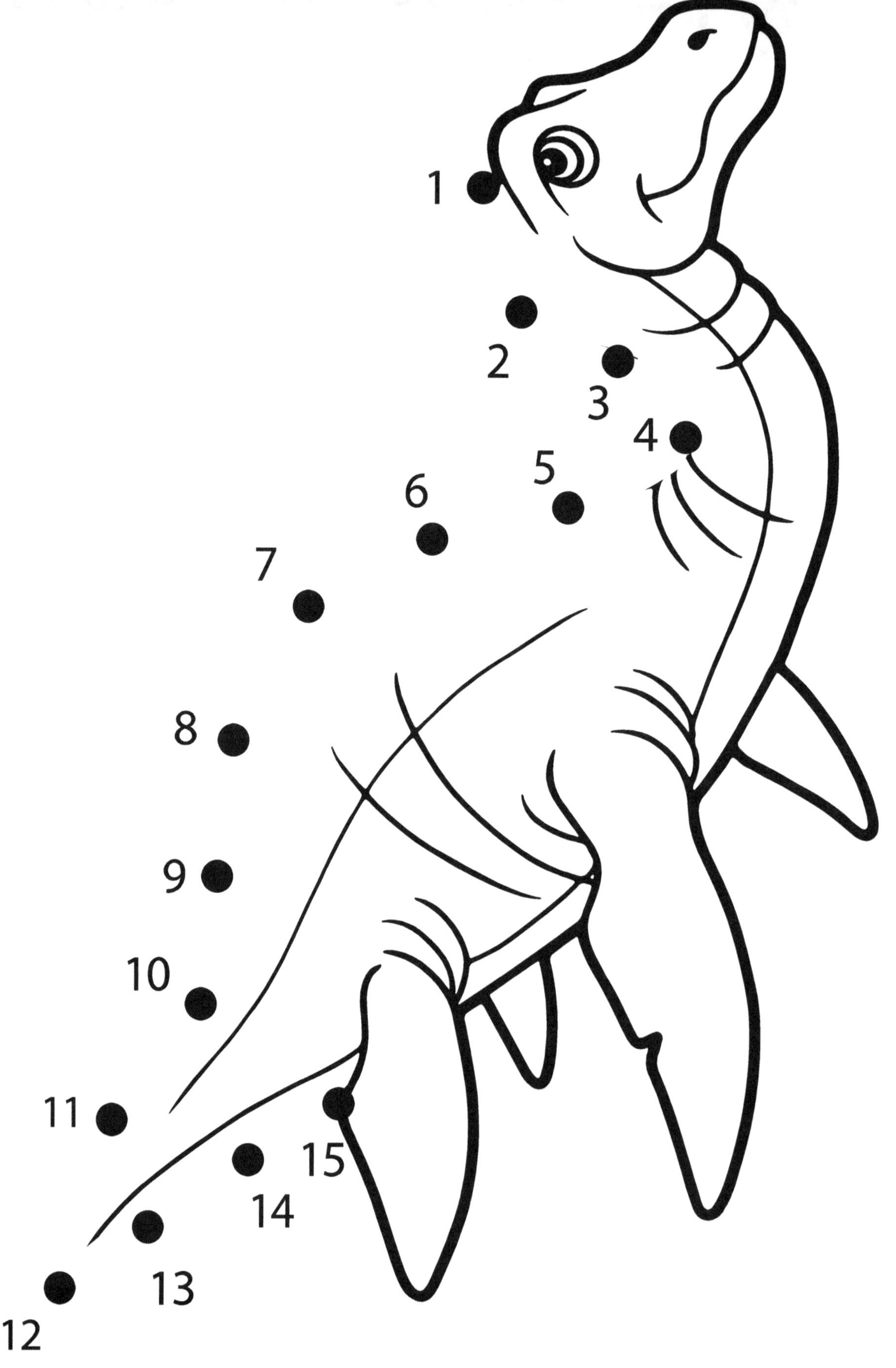

DOT - TO - DOT

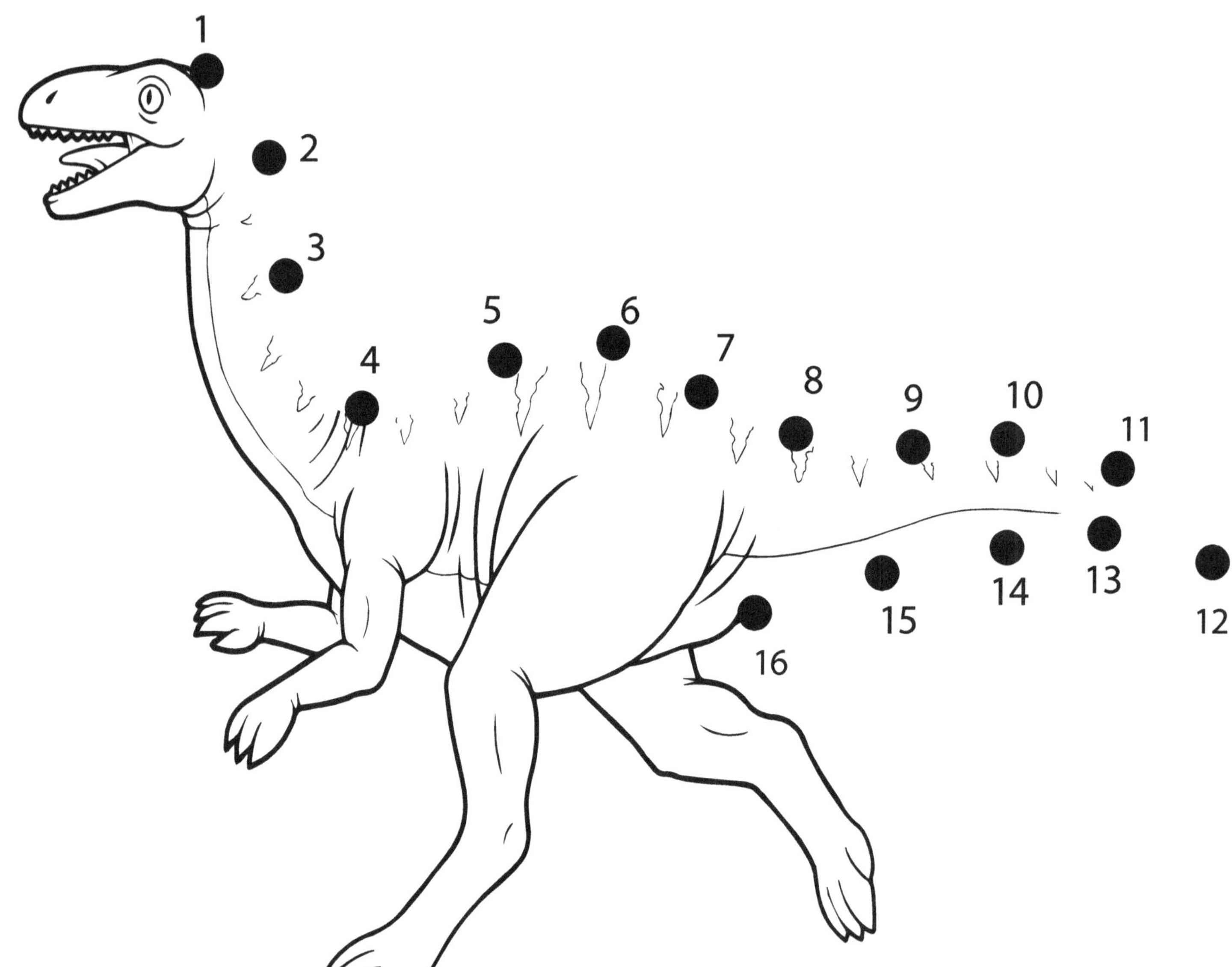

DOT - TO - DOT

DOT - TO - DOT

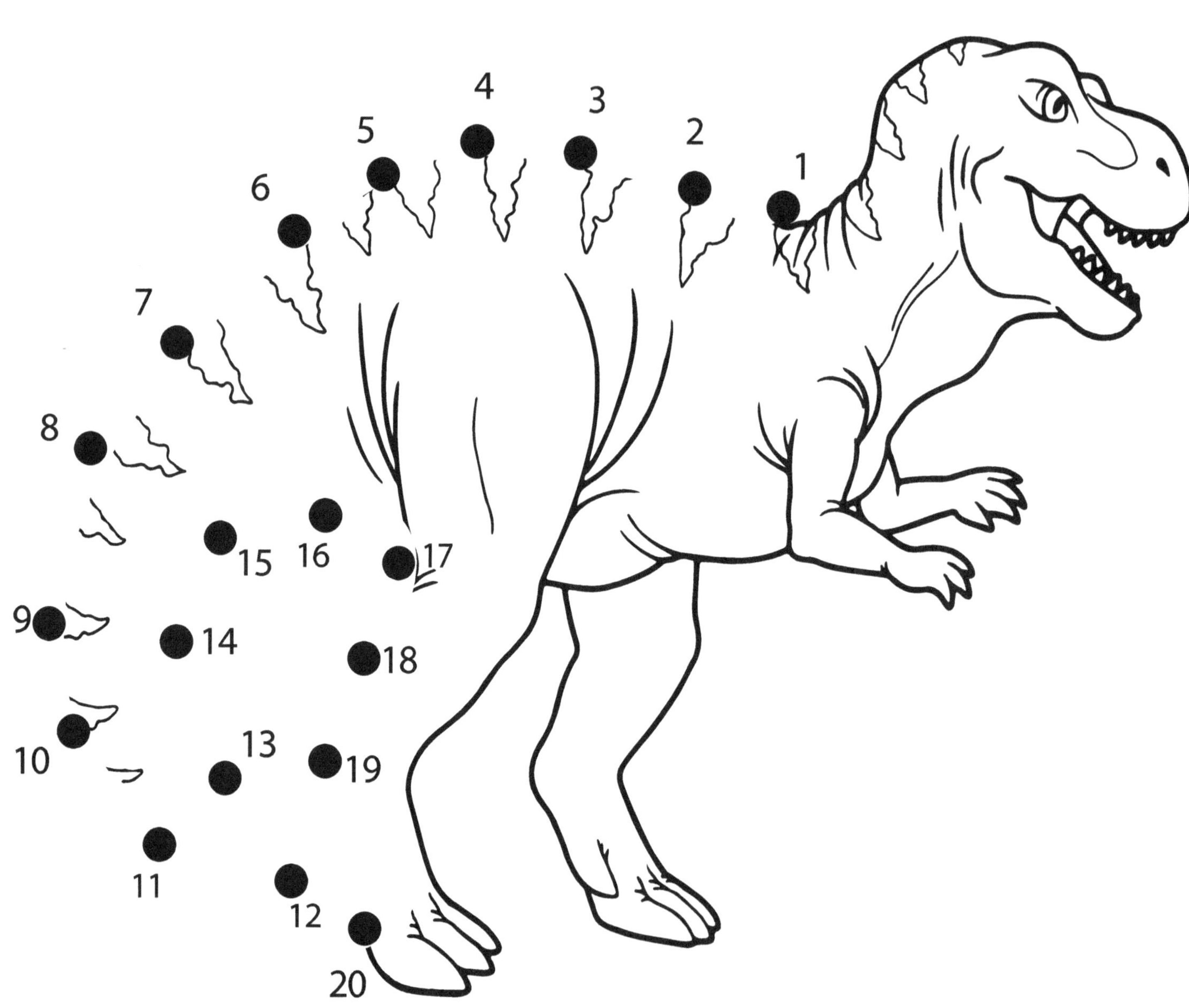

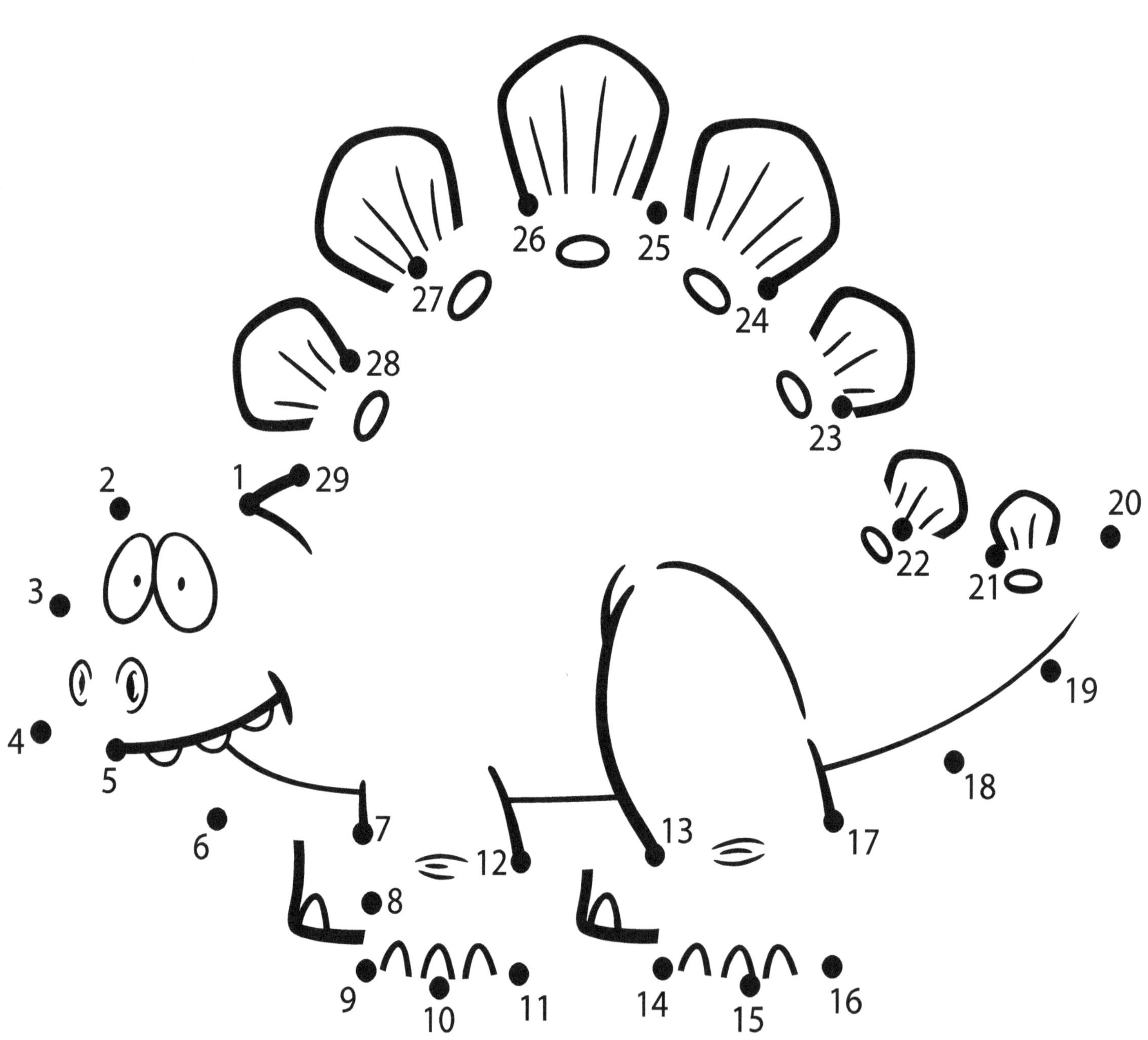

DOT - TO - DOT

DOT - TO - DOT

DOT - TO - DOT

1
2
3
4
5
6
7
8
9
10
11
12
13
14
15
16
17
18
19
20
21
22
23
24
25
26
27
28
29
30
31
32
33
34
35
36
37
38
39
40

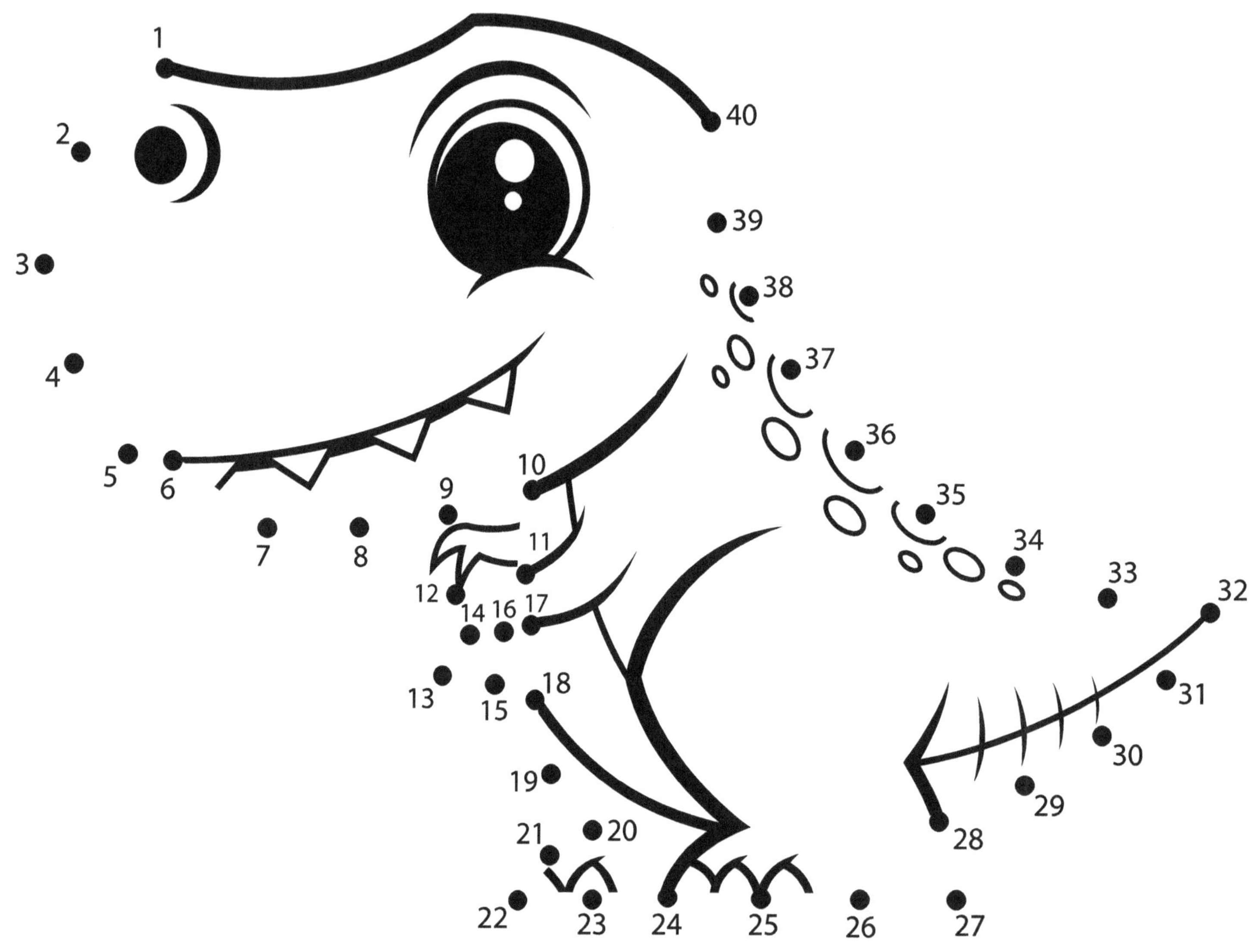

DOT - TO - DOT

DOT - TO - DOT

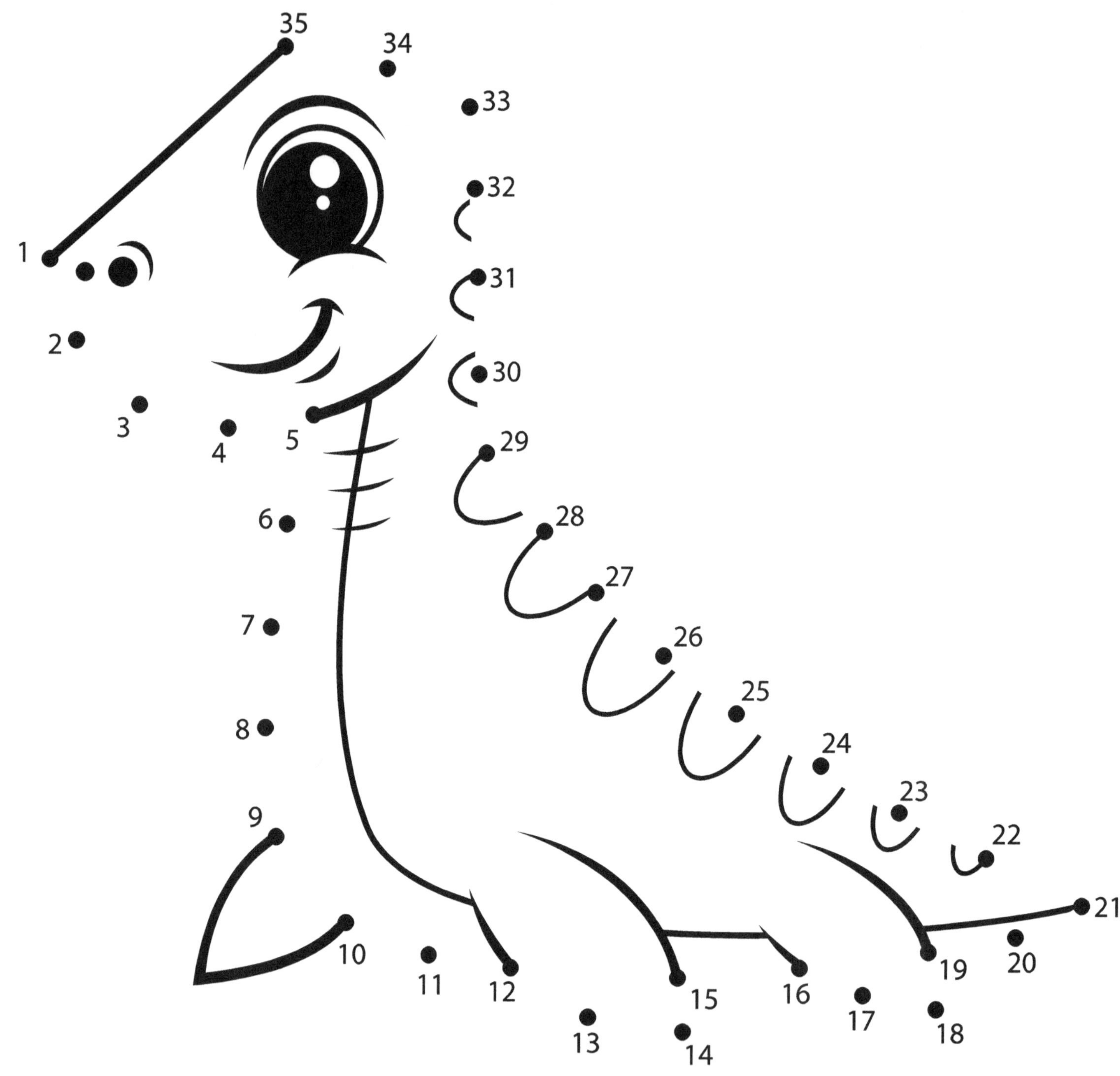

DOT - TO - DOT

DOT - TO - DOT

DOT - TO - DOT

1
2
3
4
5
6
7
8
9
10
11
12
13
14
15
16
17
18
19
20
21
22
23
24
25
26
27
28
29
30
31
32

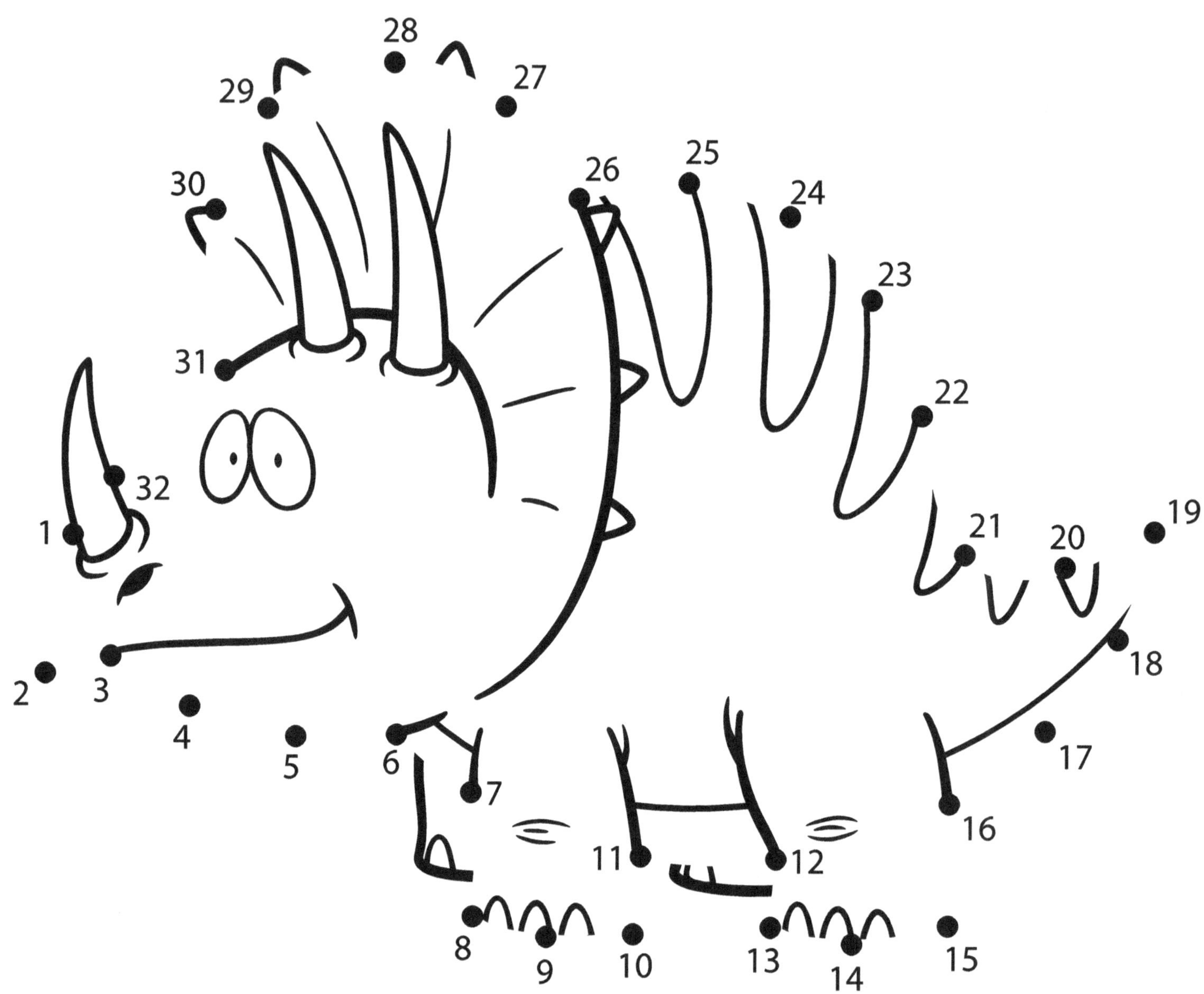

DOT - TO - DOT

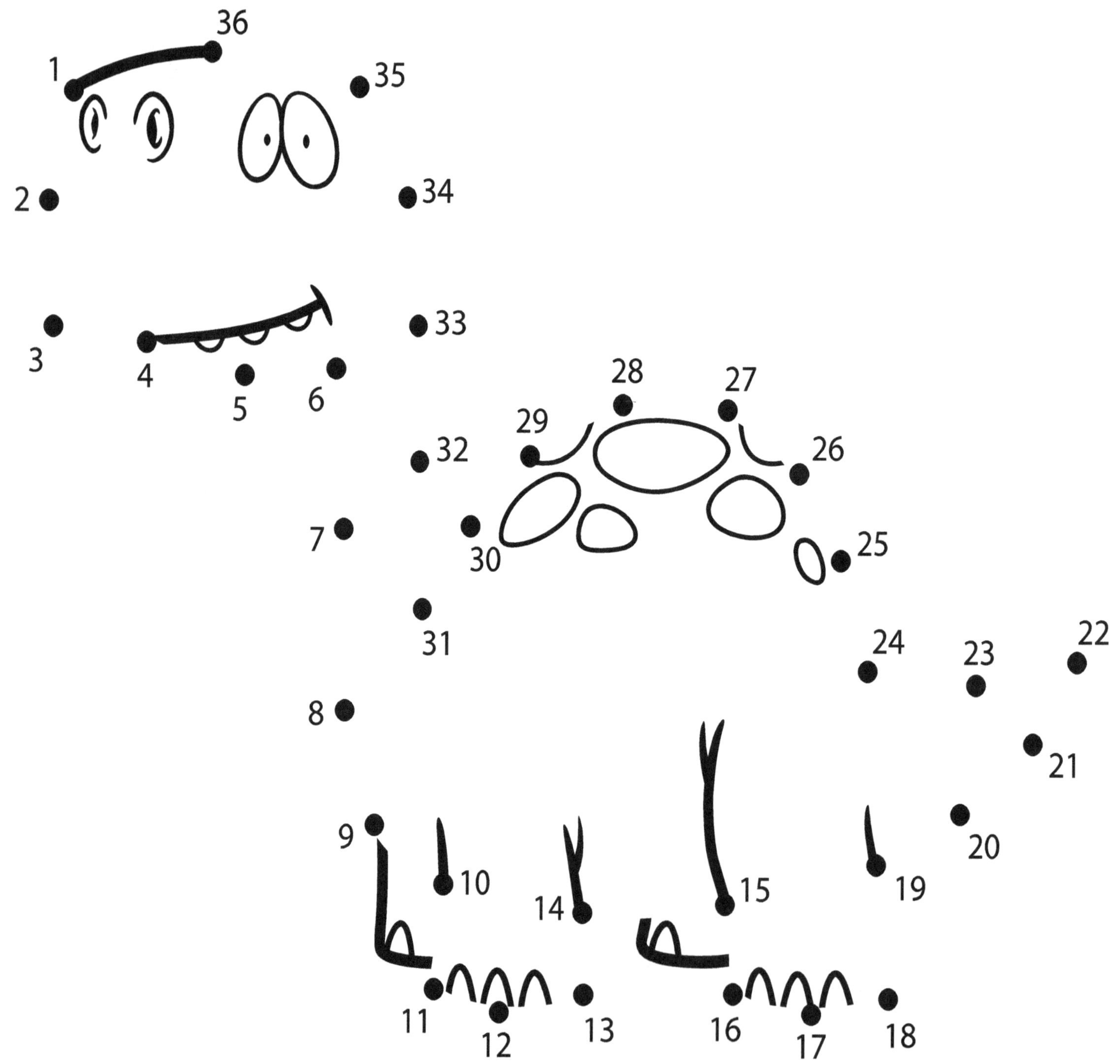

DOT - TO - DOT

DOT - TO - DOT

DOT - TO - DOT

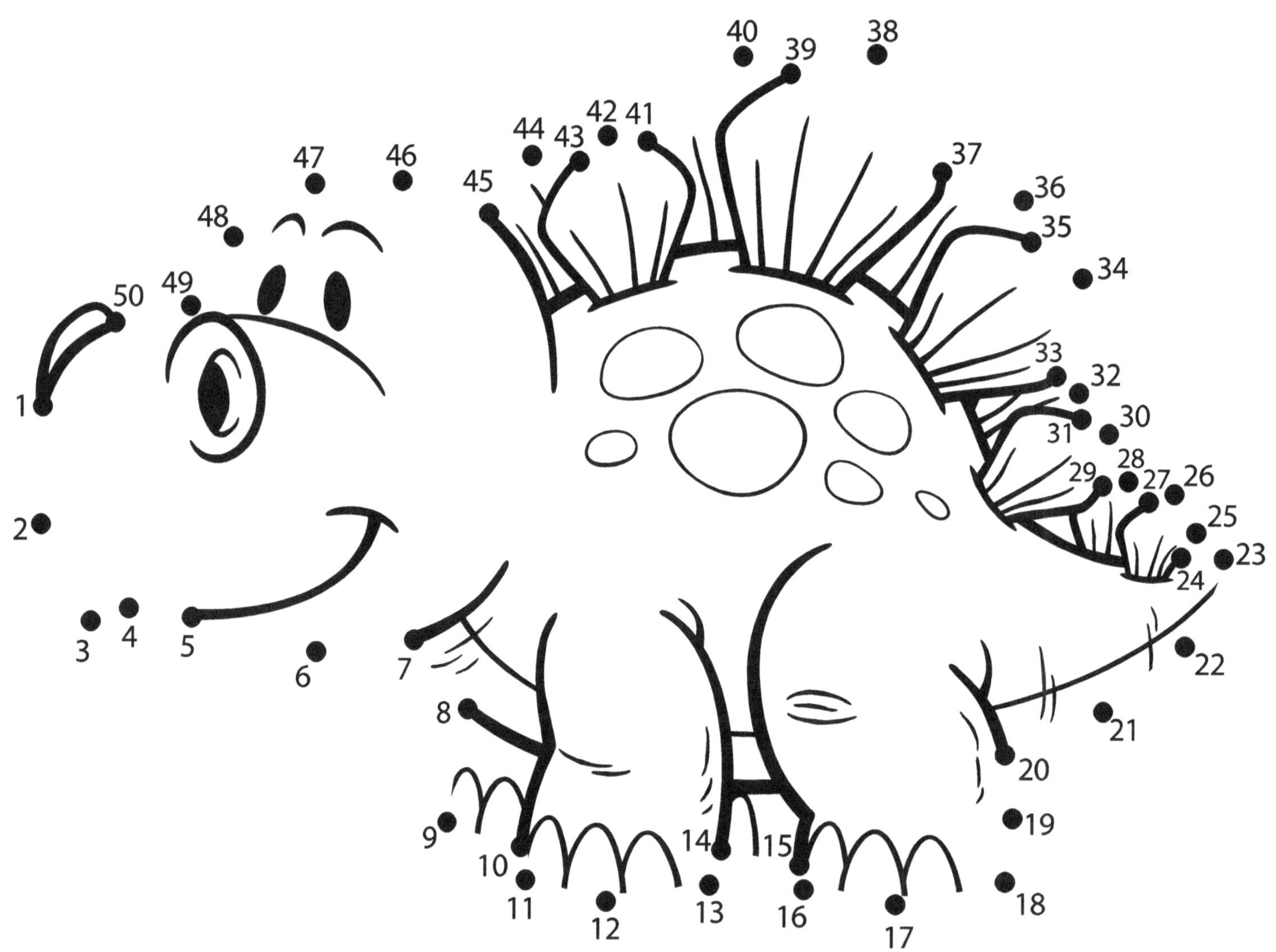

DOT - TO - DOT

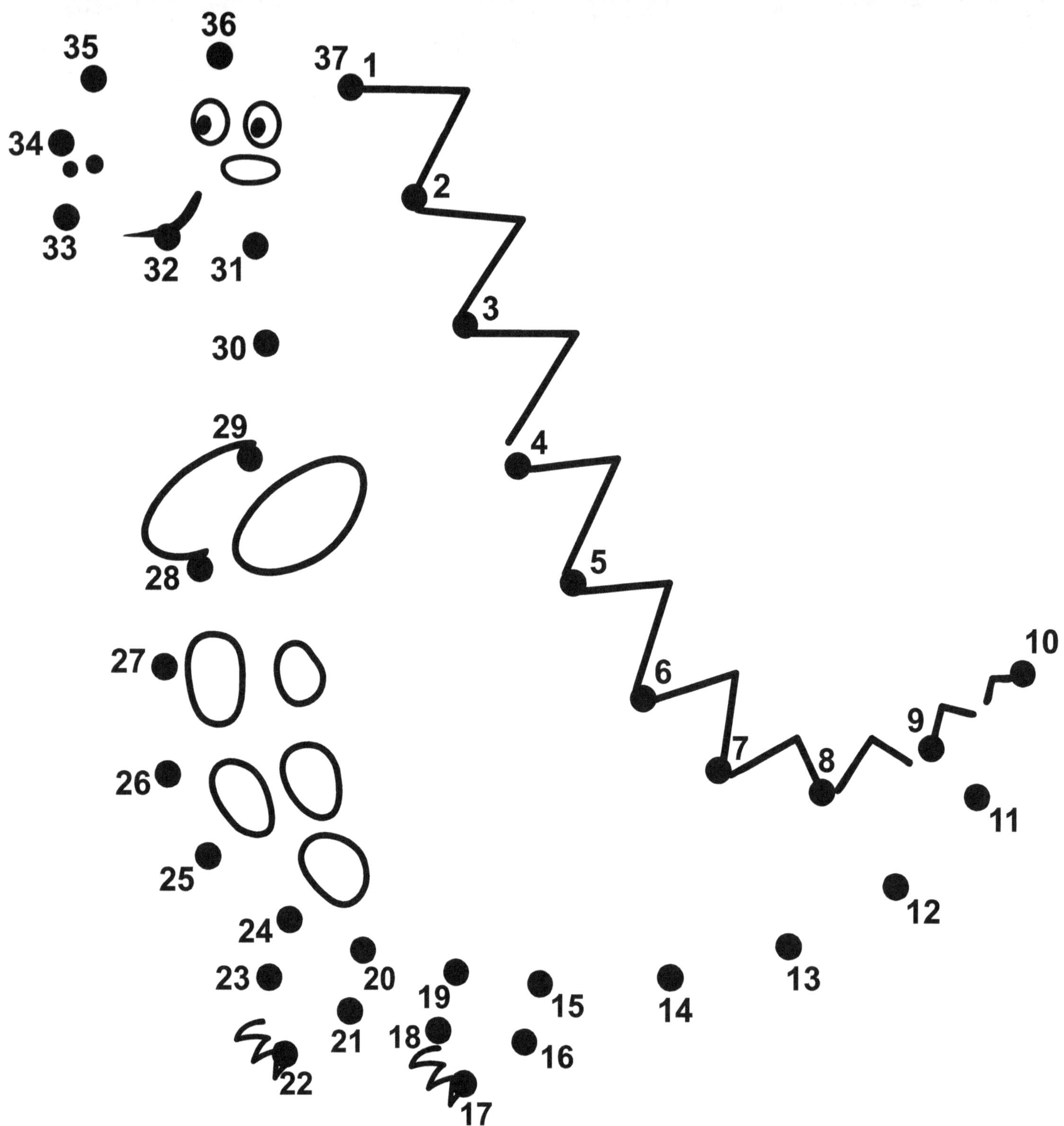

DOT - TO - DOT

if you like one of our books please don't hesitate to leave a sweet review like you.